Handwriting Without

Name:

Handwriting Without Tears®

8001 MacArthur Blvd
Cabin John, MD 20818
301.263.2700
www.hwtears.com

Authors: Jan Z. Olsen, OTR and Edith H. Fine
Illustrator: Jef Mallett, creator of the *Frazz* comic strip
HWT Adviser: Emily F. Knapton, M.Ed., OTR/L
HWT Designers: Shannon Rutledge, Julie Koborg, Leah Connor, and Frances Nefsky
Additional Illustrations by: Jan Z. Olsen and Julie Olsen

AUTHORS, ILLUSTRATOR, AND TEACHERS

Jan Z. Olsen, OTR

Jan is an occupational therapist. Her specialty is making it easy and fun for all students to learn handwriting. She originally developed the Handwriting Without Tears® program to help her own son. Now, the program helps millions of children. Jan is also an artist, but for this book, she and Edith thought Jef Mallett's cartoon characters were nifty.

Edith H. Fine

Edith loves words and writing. Her zany book, *CrytoMania!*, transports kids into Greek and Latin. She has co-authored two wildly popular grammar guides, *Nitty-Gritty Grammar* and *More Nitty-Gritty Grammar*. Other books include *Under the Lemon Moon*, *Cricket at the Manger*, and *Armando and the Blue Tarp School*, and *Water, Weed, and Wait*. edithfine.com

Jef Mallett

Jef is an award-winning cartoonist, as well as an author and pet lover. He started a daily comic strip when he was just 15 years old. His *Frazz* comic strip was launched in 2001 and now runs in 200 newspapers. Jef is also the author of *Dangerous Dan*, a children's book.

Credit: Kim Kauffman Photography

ɔdago

dago the Magician became nous by turning a herd of phants into a flock of chickens. he started by changing magic c the letters a, o, d, g, and q.

Racing Robin

Racing Robin is a track star. She coaches children, showing them how to keep printing fast and neat.

Dr. Less

Maura Less writes spine-tingling mysteries. She is a stickler for grammar.

Diver Dave

Diver Dave loves the water. He likes to dive perfectly straight down. He'll take you deep into the alphabet with the diver letters: p, r, n, m, h, and b.

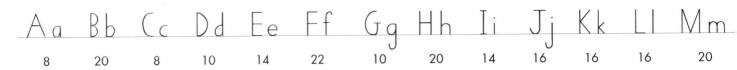
TABLE OF CONTENTS

INTRODUCTION

PRINTING - **Fast and Neat**

PRINTING & GRAMMAR - **Did she say Gramma?**

Nn Oo Pp Qq Rr Ss Tt Uu Vv Ww Xx Yy Zz

PRINTING & GRAMMAR - Continued

PRINTING WITH LATIN & GREEK - It's All Greek to Me!

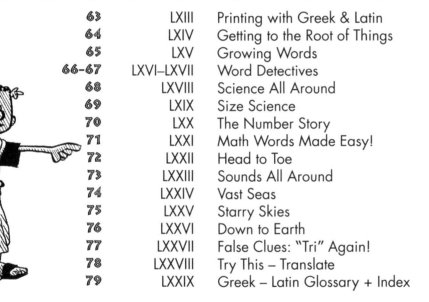

PRINTING & THE WRITER'S NOTEBOOK

For Teachers

Can-Do Print - About this workbook

Can-Do Print is designed for 5th graders or older students who want to improve their printing. This workbook is also for you, a busy teacher who may not have been trained to teach handwriting. You can teach straight from this workbook. Just read this information, and stay a day ahead of your students as you follow the directions on each page.

What's Inside?

Can-Do Print is organized in four sections. The first section teaches and reviews print. The next three sections use print in fun, interesting ways to develop writing skills.

PRINTING
Teach lowercase letters and words.

GRAMMAR
Teach capitals, grammar, and punctuation.

LATIN & GREEK
Build reading and vocabulary skills.

WRITER'S NOTEBOOK
Teach a variety of writing styles.

PRINTING - Fast and Neat

Model how to form the letters. Watch your students and help them check their work. Personal styles are fine, but the steps must follow the workbook. Consistent, correct habits promote neat and fast printing. Immediately after the printing lessons is a surprise. This workbook has tips for reading cursive and you'll notice many "Change *cursive* to print" activities.

GRAMMAR - Did she say Gramma?

Capital letters are taught in formation groups to promote efficient, neat printing. At the same time, students get a grammar boost with Edith Fine's fresh approach and Jef Mallett's cartoons. Your students will like this new twist on the parts of speech, pronoun cases, quotations, etc.

LATIN & GREEK - It's All Greek to Me!

Big words are not intimidating when students know a little Latin and Greek. Your students will learn how to figure out roots, prefixes, and suffixes as they polish their printing. The range of subjects extends from constellations to orthodontists. Here's a vocabulary and knowledge boost.

WRITER'S NOTEBOOK

Bring in the professionals! Mark Twain, Frederick Douglass, Emily Dickinson and other famous writers are here to inspire and coach your students in writing poetry, diaries, plays, short stories, etc. This final section gives extensive printing practice while promoting different writing genres.

The FINE Print: A play on words with the co-author's name, Edith FINE, gives interesting information and tips. Sometimes the content is advanced instruction and sometimes it's just fun. Look for this bonus at the bottom of many pages.

For Teachers

How do I use this book?

Start by teaching the first 42 pages in order. Those pages have the printing lessons. After that, you may teach pages out of order to complement your other instruction. Some pages may take two or more days to complete. Plan to spend 10 to 15 minutes each day. There is no hurry.

What's In Style?

Can-Do Print uses a simple vertical print. If your students have or develop a style that *slants* or is fancier, that's fine. What's important is that they use correct letter formation habits.

Lines and Size This book promotes a size that is appropriate for writing on regular ruled notebook paper. This first section, Printing - Fast and Neat, uses a version of Handwriting Without Tears® double lines that has a solid black baseline and a faint gray midline. It helps students make letters a consistent size and place tall, small, and descending letters correctly. After the first section, students write on single lines.

Teach and Check

Show students how to check their own and each other's work. The goal is for your whole class to write well. It is fine for them to check, coach, and help each other (See page 6 for futher details). Here is what they check:

☑ **Check Letter**
1. Start correctly.
2. Do each step.
3. Bump the lines.

☑ **Check Word**
1. Make letters the right size.
2. Place letters correctly.
3. Put letters close.

☑ **Check Sentence**
1. Start with a capital.
2. Put space between words.
3. Use punctuation.

READING CURSIVE The selection of this workbook indicates a preference for printing. But, students still need to know how to read other people's cursive writing. This section includes some quick tips to make it easier.

Review and Mastery: Cursive to Print

After the printing lessons, there is a translation activity on pp. 26–27. Students change cursive letters and words into print. When you check those pages, you will see if there are any letters that need review. It's fine for students to use the page references for independent review too.

pages
20–21   *m   h   b   marine   harbor   bubble*
          m   h   b   marine   harbor   bubble

 Extra Practice: Give students extra cursive practice outside the workbook. When you see this image, you'll find ideas for more writing activities. Use these or make up your own. It's important that students use their print skills after they've learned them.

For Students

Can-Do Print - About this workbook

This is an advanced workbook for you, a student who prefers printing to cursive. The lessons are designed to make your printing look neater and more grown up. If you follow the tips about starting letters at the top, you'll find that you can print faster and still have neat work. (Lowercase **d** and **e** are the only letters that don't start at the top).

What's inside?

The first part of the book teaches or reviews letters and words. After that, there are three more sections. In those sections, you'll practice neat printing as you learn other interesting things.

PRINTING

GRAMMAR

LATIN & GREEK

WRITER'S NOTEBOOK

What's In Style, Printing or Cursive?

In 1776, John Hancock signed the Declaration of Independence very large so that King George III of England would notice his signature.

Your parents and grandparents probably learned to print first.

Later, they probably learned a cursive style like this.

It isn't important whether your style is like John Hancock's, your parents', or mine. It is important that you form the letters correctly and consistently, and that everyone can easily read your writing.

Can-Do Print uses an efficient, vertical style that is easy to learn, easy to write, and easy to read. Enjoy refining your print. This book will help make your printing fast and neat.

Jan Z. Olsen

For Students

Learn and Check
Learn letters, words, sentences, and how to check them.
When you see the box ☐, it's time to check your work.

 Check letter Teachers: Help children ✓ their letter for correct Start, Steps, and Bump.

1. Start correctly.   **2.** Do each step.   **3.** Bump the lines.

  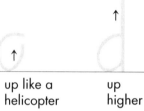 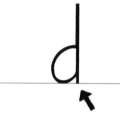

Magic c   up like a   up   down
            helicopter   higher bump

 Check word Teachers: Help children ✓ their word for correct letter Size, Placement, and Closeness.

1. Make letters the right size.
2. Place letters correctly - tall, small, or descending.   **3.** Put letters close.

Tall   **Small**   **Descending**

 Check sentence Teachers: Help children ✓ their sentence for correct Capitalization, Word Spacing, and Ending Punctuation.

1. Start with a capital.   **2.** Put space between words.   **3.** End with . ? or !

I will have finished by noon.

PRINTING - Fast and Neat

How about some Magic **c** madness first?
Watch how **c** can turn into **o** or **a**.

Codago the Magician

c o a

☑ Check Letter

1. Start correctly.
2. Do each step.
3. Bump the lines.

Trace the steps.

Write the letter. ☐ Write & Check C

C   Magic c

☐ Write & Check C

O   Magic c   keep on   stop
                        going

☐ Write & Check a

a   Magic c   up like a   touch   down
                        helicopter   bump

© 2013 Handwriting Without Tea

Copy the letters. Start on the dots.

C   ·   C   ·   C   ·   C   ·

O   ·   O   ·   O   ·   O   ·

a   ·   a   ·   a   ·   a   ·

Copy below the model.

C   cocoa   cocoa   cocoa

Hey — cocoa? This is crazy, we can't write many words with only these 3 letters.

Yeah, I'd like to write **goat**, but we don't have **g** or **t** yet.

Whoosh, we can't do **cat**, we don't have **t** yet.

No, no, we can't write **dog** yet, we don't have **d** or **g**.

Codago the Magician

Yes, you are right, **d** and **g** are Magic **c** letters too.

d g t

☑ Check Letter
1. Start correctly.
2. Do each step.
3. Bump the lines.

Trace the steps.

Write the letter. ☐ Write & Check **d**

d — Magic c — up like a helicopter — up higher — down bump

☐ Write & Check **g**

g — Magic c — up touch — back down — turn

Time for **t**!

☐ Write & Check **t**

t — down — cross — Note: Left-handed students may cross t like this ←.

© 2013 Handwriting Without Tear

Copy the letters. Start on the dots.

d   ·   d   ·   d   ·   d   ·

g   ·   g   ·   g   ·   g   ·

A **t**? This **t** isn't a Magic **c** letter but it sure can help me make some good words.

t   ·   t   ·   t   ·

☑ Check Word

1. Make letters the right size.
2. Place letters correctly.
3. Put letters close.

Copy below the model.

Check the word.

d   dog   dot   data   dodo

☐ Check dodo

g   goat   goo   good   gag

☐ Check gag

t   too   taco   toga   toad

☐ Check toad

Six letters aren't enough. Turn the page and Coach Racing Robin will get you moving.

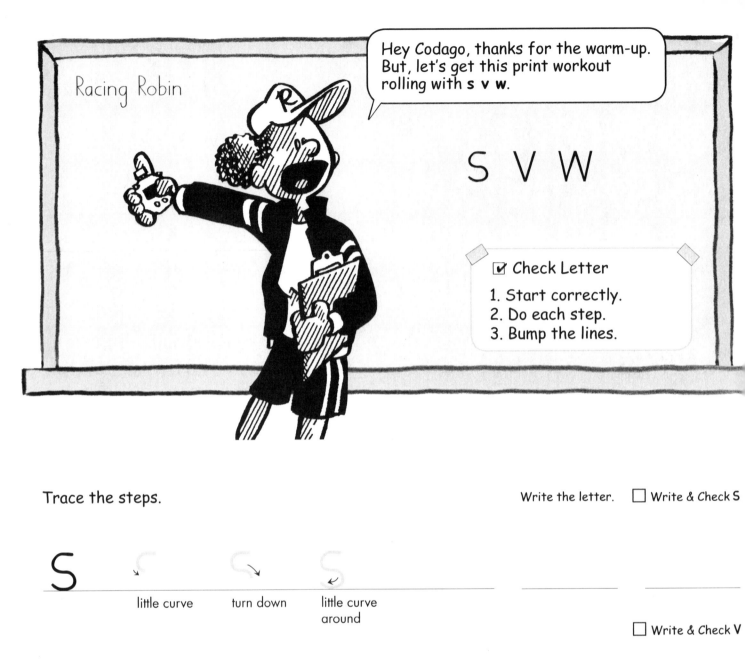

Racing Robin

Hey Codago, thanks for the warm-up. But, let's get this print workout rolling with **s v w**.

S V W

☑ **Check Letter**
1. Start correctly.
2. Do each step.
3. Bump the lines.

Trace the steps.   Write the letter. ☐ Write & Check **S**

S   little curve   turn down   little curve around

☐ Write & Check **V**

V   slide down   slide up

☐ Write & Check **W**

W   slide down and up   do it again

Copy the letters. Start on the dots.

s · s · s · s ·

v · v · v · v ·

w · w · w · w ·

It's amazing! We can make some great words with only these nine letters:
coa   dgt   svw

Copy below the model.

Check the word.

s   soda   stow   swag   scoot

☐ Check SCOOT

v   vat   vast   vow   vows

☐ Check VOWS

w   wag   wads   watts   woods

☐ Check WOODS

Dr. Less

Coach Robin, don't go too fast. We need to add some vowels.

u i e

Trace the steps.

Write the letter.   ☐ Write & Check u

u

down
travel
up

slide down
bump

☐ Write & Check i

i

dot

down

☐ Write & Check e

e

start   hit the ball   run the bases   3 stop

Copy the letters. Start on the dots.

u ·   u ·   u ·   u ·

i ·   i ·   i ·   i ·

e ·   e ·   e ·   e ·

Learning these vowels is wonderful.
We can make some interesting words.
Look at these - **vicissitude, devastated.**

☑ Check Word

1. Make letters the right size.
2. Place letters correctly.
3. Put letters close.

Copy below the model.

Check the word.

u   us   use   used   usage

☐ Check **usage**

i   ice   idea   ivied   iota

☐ Check **iota**

e   ease   edge   ewe   edit

☐ Check **edit**

For fun, try one:

vicissitude   devastated

Racing Robin

Time for consonants! Ooops, **y** can be a vowel too.

l k y j

Trace the steps.

l
down

k
down   kick!   slide away

y
slide down   slide down lower

j
down   down lower   turn   dot

Write the letter.   ☐ Write & Check l

☐ Write & Check k

☐ Write & Check y

☐ Write & Check j

Copy the letters. Start on the dots.

l　　　l　　　l　　　l

k　　　k　　　k　　　k

y　　　y　　　y　　　y

j　　　j　　　j　　　j

Finish the workout with these great words, and then you're off to dive with Diver Dave. He'll take you deep into the alphabet.

Copy below the model.

Check the word.

l　　leg　　lose　　lost　　league

☐ Check **league**

k　　kick　　kudos　　kayak　　kite

☐ Check **kite**

y　　yes　　yoga　　yield　　yellow

☐ Check **yellow**

j　　joy　　judo　　jockey　　justice

☐ Check **justice**

Diver Dave

The next six letters are all diver letters. Dive down straight, come up straight, and then swim to the side. Let's start practicing diver letters with **p r** and **n**.

p r n

Trace the steps.

Write the letter. ☐ Write & Check p

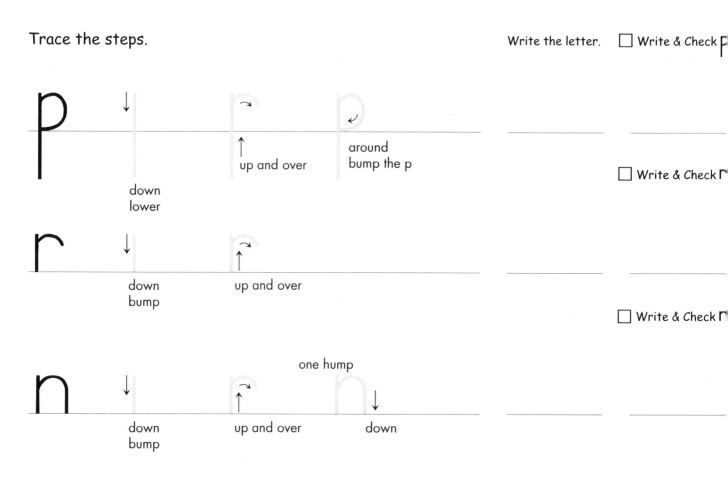

p
↓ down lower
↗ ↑ up and over
↩ around bump the p

☐ Write & Check r

r
↓ down bump
↗ ↑ up and over

☐ Write & Check n

n
↓ down bump
↗ ↑ up and over
one hump
↓ down

Copy the letters. Start on the dots.

p   p   p   p

r   r   r   r

n   n   n   n

Remember to dive straight down and come straight back up. Here are some watery words to print.

Copy below the model.

Check the word.

p   pour   plank   pontoon   paddle

☐ Check **paddle**

r   river   run   row   rudder

☐ Check **rudder**

n   navy   nautical   navigate   nap

☐ Check **nap**

There are just three more diver letters, **m h b**. Learning these will be smooth, like my head.

Diver Dave

m h b

Trace the steps.

Write the letter. ☐ Write & Check m

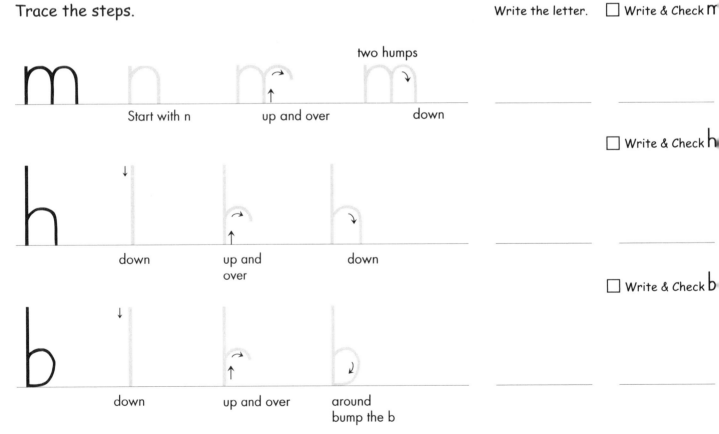

two humps

m n m m

Start with n | up and over | down

☐ Write & Check h

h

down | up and over | down

☐ Write & Check b

b

down | up and over | around bump the b

Copy the letters. Start on the dots.

m ⋅   m ⋅   m ⋅   m ⋅

n ⋅   h ⋅   h ⋅   h ⋅

b ⋅   b ⋅   b ⋅   b ⋅

Blup, blup, blup, blup, blup. . .
Remember! For diver letters, you need
to dive down, come up, and swim over.

Copy below the model.

Check the word.

m   mast   mermaid   maroon   marine

☐ Check **marine**

h   harbor   helm   harpoon   hoist

☐ Check **hoist**

b   boom   bayou   bubble   ballast

☐ Check **ballast**

Racing Robin

Great job! You've made it to the end. We'll finish up with **f q x z.**

f q x z

Trace the steps.

f f f f

up
and down   cross

Write the letter. ☐ Write & Check f

☐ Write & Check q

q q q q q

Magic c   up   back
               touch   down

                                   U turn

☐ Write & Check X

X X X

slide down   slide down

☐ Write & Check Z

Z Z Z

across   slide down   across

Copy the letters. Start on the dots.

f ·   f ·   f ·   f ·

q ·   q ·   q ·   q ·

x ·   x ·   x ·   x ·

z ·   z ·   z ·   z ·

Congratulations!
You've done great work!

Copy below the model.

f   fine   finish   fabulous   form

☐ Check **form**

q   quiet   quaint   quibble   queen

☐ Check **queen**

x   xerox   x-ray   xylophone   xylem

☐ Check **xylem**

z   zoo   zebra   zinnia   zipper

☐ Check **zipper**

READING CURSIVE

You have decided to stick with printing. That's great, but we want to give you a hand with reading other people's cursive writing.

Here's the cursive alphabet:

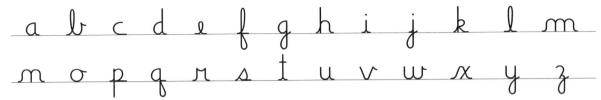

Let's try some translating from cursive to print.

SUPER EASY – Here are the cursive letters that look almost identical to print.
Change cursive to print.

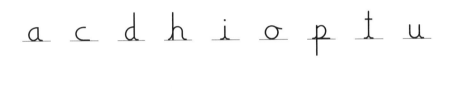

_ _ _ _ _ _ _ _ _

EASY – Here are the cursive letters that look very close to print.
Change cursive to print.

_ _ _ _ _ _ _

A LITTLE TRICKY – Here are some letters that can be a little tricky.
Change cursive to print.

_ _ _ _ _ _ _ _ _ _ _ _

In the rest of the book, you'll get to learn the cursive capitals. But, here are some quick tips:
The most frequently used capitals at the beginning of sentences or questions: T = J, I = ℐ, W = W.
And, here are the strangest looking cursive capitals G = D, Q = 2, S = 8, Z = ℨ.

Now that you have seen all 26 lowercase letters, let's dig into some of the weird things that happen in cursive. We'll give you tricks to figure them out.

TRICK 1
Focus on the main part of the letter and not the connection start or ending.
Change *cursive* to print.

attach   *doodad*   *potato*

_____   _____   _____

TRICK 2
Don't let people who have slanted, loopy, or extravagant styles throw you off. Just imagine the letters straight or tilt the paper. Then focus on the main part of the letter and not the connection.

This is what it would look like if you tilted the paper. See how the letters look straight and are easier to read.

TRICK 3
Cursive letter **o w b v** end high. Letters that come after **o**, **w**, **b**, or **v** must start high. Sometimes that changes the look of the cursive letter. If a letter looks funny to you, it's probably one of these letters that's been changed to start high.

Change *cursive* to print.

_____   _____   _____   _____   _____   _____

TRICK 4
The size of letters can be a clue. Cursive and print are the same size, except for letters **f** and **z**.
Change *cursive* to print.

Small: *ace*   *rum*   *mam*   *was*   *use*

_____   _____   _____   _____   _____

Tall: *but*   *dot*   *let*   *hid*

The only letters that don't match in size are:

f = f   *z* = z

_____   _____   _____   _____

Descending: 

_____   _____   _____   _____

Review and Mastery: Cursive to Print

Translate — Not Spanish, French, or Chinese. You will translate cursive into print.

Change cursive to print. Write below the models.

pages
8–9
c   o   a   coo   cocoa

pages
10–11
d   g   t   dog   goat   taco

pages
12–13
s   v   w   soda   vast   woods

pages
14–15
u   i   e   used   idea   edge

Review and Mastery: Cursive to Print

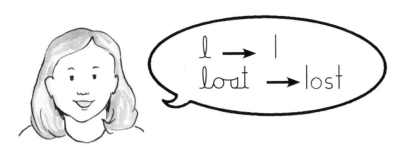

Change cursive to print. Write below the models.

pages
16–17   *l*   *k*   *y*   *j*   *lost*   *kick*   *yoga*   *judo*

pages
18–19   *p*   *r*   *n*   *plank*   *river*   *nap*

pages
20–21   *m*   *h*   *b*   *marine*   *harbor*   *bubble*

pages
22–23   *f*   *q*   *x*   *z*   *fine*   *quiet*   *x-ray*   *zebra*

The FINE Print   Teachers and students, check these pages. Brush up on any needed letters or words. There are additional practice pages for refining print skills on our website, www.hwtears.com in the Classroom Extras section.

PRINTING & GRAMMAR - Did she say Gramma?

GET READY FOR CAPITALS AND GRAMMAR.

DID SHE SAY "GRAMMA"?

START CAPITALS

A B C D E F G H I J K L M
N O P Q R S T U V W X Y Z

START GRAMMAR

Grammar has two **a**'s, just like Gr**a**mm**a**! The rules for speaking and writing a language are called grammar. Here are some basic grammar rules.

1. A sentence expresses a complete thought. **I write words.**
2. Sentences have two parts: the subject and the predicate.
   - The subject "**I**" tells who or what the sentence is about.
   - The predicate "**write words**" tells what the subject is or what the subject is doing.
3. Sentences start with capital letters.
4. Sentences stop with a **.** **!** or ?

EIGHT PARTS OF SPEECH

WORDS AND THEIR JOBS – 8 PARTS OF SPEECH

Words work. They have jobs. There are 8 jobs. Here is a fun way to learn how words work. Practice reading cursive.

1. **Nouns**   give you a <u>name</u>.

2. **Adjectives**   make you <u>smart</u> and <u>good looking</u>.

3. **Pronouns**   let <u>you</u> talk about <u>yourself</u>. "<u>I</u> am the <u>one</u>. Look at <u>me</u>."

4. **Verbs**   <u>make</u> you what you <u>are</u>. Verbs also <u>make</u> you <u>run</u> and <u>think</u>.

5. **Adverbs**   help you run <u>quickly</u>, and <u>always</u> think <u>brilliantly</u>.

6. **Prepositions** put you <u>before</u> other people, <u>on</u> top <u>of</u> the world.

7. **Conjunctions** put this <u>and</u> that together, <u>or</u> apart, <u>but</u> it's your choice.

8. **Interjections** say, "<u>Gee whiz</u>!"

PARTS OF SPEECH

Below are some examples. Now, you write two more.

1. Nouns	bus	man		
2. Adjectives	large	young		
3. Pronouns	she	they		
4. Verbs	write	run		
5. Adverbs	slowly	never		
6. Prepositions	in	under		
7. Conjunctions		or		
8. Interjections	Oh no!	Golly!		

The FINE Print   Here is another way to learn how words work. **It is the 8 Parts of Speech.**

1. <u>Nouns</u>   name people, places, things, or ideas.
2. <u>Adjectives</u>   describe nouns or pronouns.
3. <u>Pronouns</u>   take the place of nouns.
4. <u>Verbs</u>   show actions or state of being.
5. <u>Adverbs</u>   describe verbs, adjectives, or other adverbs.
6. <u>Prepositions</u>   show position in time or space.
7. <u>Conjunctions</u>   join words or groups of words.
8. <u>Interjections</u>   show emotion with one or two words.

WORDS WORK

ONE WORD CAN DO DIFFERENT JOBS

Words are amazing. They can do many different jobs. Take the word, "paint."

I paint.   Paint is a verb.

yellow paint   Paint is a common noun.

The pony's name is Paint.   Paint is a proper noun.

WORDS CAN CHANGE CLOTHES TO DO OTHER JOBS

Words can change. They can even get help to do more jobs.
Take paint and add -ed = painted. Write __painted__ on the lines in print.

a _____ door   Painted is an adjective.

I _____ .   Painted is a past tense verb.

I have _____ all day. With helping "have," painted is a perfect verb.

Take paint and add -ing = painting. Write __painting__ on the lines in print.

a _____ of a dog   Painting is a noun.

a _____ lesson   Painting is an adjective.

I am _____ .   With helping "am," painting is a verb.

WORDS AGREE WITH EACH OTHER

Subjects and verbs must agree. Write the right verb: am are is

I _____.   You_____.   Joshua_____.   She_____.

Subjects and verbs must agree. Write the right verb: run runs

I _____.   You_____.   He_____.   Maya_____.

STARTING AND STOPPING PUNCTUATION . ? !

STARTING AND STOPPING PUNCTUATION . ? !
Start sentences with a capital letter.
Stop with a period, exclamation point, or question mark.

SENTENCE TYPES
Declarative sentences make a statement. They end with a ⊙.
Make up an ending to the sentence. Stop with a period.

An ambulance _____

Interrogative sentences ask a question. They end with a ❓.
Make up endings to the questions. Stop with a question mark.

Who _____

What _____

When _____

Where _____

Exclamatory sentences show strong emotion. They end with an ⚠.
Change cursive to print. Rewrite these exclamations in print. Stop with an exclamation point.

Watch out for the snake!   *A snake is loose!*

_____   _____

Imperative sentences are bossy. They make a request or give an order.
Change cursive to print. Rewrite the imperative sentence in print. Stop with an exclamation point.

Call an ambulance!

☑ **Check Sentence**

1. Start with a capital.
2. Put space between words.
3. Use punctuation.

       ☐ Check Sentence

The FINE Print   In England, a period is called a full stop.
           Sometimes a subject is missing from a sentence, but you can figure it out. "Watch out!" means "**You** watch out."

COMMON NOUNS

people, places, things

If you can picture something, it's usually a **noun**.
Common nouns name people, places, or things.
Proper nouns name specific people, places, or things.

Draw a person, maybe a teacher.	Draw a place, maybe a beach.	Draw a thing, maybe an easy chair.

PEOPLE　　　　　　　　　　**PLACES**　　　　　　　　　　**THINGS**

Change cursive to print. Rewrite these common nouns in print below the models.

artist	apartment	apron
clown	city	chair
usher	universe	umbrella
yodeler	yard	yo-yo
zoologist	zoo	zebra

Cursive   Print   Start on the dot.
Make a big line down.
Jump back to the dot. Finish.

F   F   F   F   F   ☐ Write & Check **F**

E   E   E   E   E   ☐ Write & Check **E**

D   D   D   D   D   ☐ Write & Check **D**

P   P   P   P   P   ☐ Write & Check **P**

B   B   B   B   B   ☐ Write & Check **B**

R   R   R   R   R   ☐ Write & Check **R**

N   N   N   N   N   ☐ Write & Check **N**

M   M   M   M   M   ☐ Write & Check **M**

Change cursive to print.

B   D   E   F   M   N   P   R

The FINE Print   There are additional practice pages for refining print skills on our website, www.hwtears.com in the Classroom Extras section.

PROPER NOUNS

Cursive   Print

Start on the dot.
Make a big line down.
Finish.

K   K   K   K   ☐ Write & Check

L   L   L   L   ☐ Write & Check

U   U   U   U   ☐ Write & Check

PROPER NOUNS

Names of specific people are proper nouns. Capitalize people's names.
Copy the proper nouns. Use a capital.

Kayo   Kimberly   Kyle

Lawrence   Lucia   Latisha

Ursula   Ulrich   Ulysses

Draw a picture of what you imagine Lucia and Kyle look like.

Lucia

Kyle

PROPER NOUNS

ASY CAPITALS

Cursive   Print   Start on the dot.

V V · V · V · ☐ Write & Check **V**

W W · W · W · ☐ Write & Check **W**

X X · X · X · ☐ Write & Check **X**

y y · y · y · ☐ Write & Check **Y**

z Z · Z · Z · ☐ Write & Check **Z**

PROPER NOUNS

Name of specific places are proper nouns.
Copy below the models. Start with a capital.

Venezuela   Vancouver   Virginia

Wyoming   Washington   Wisconsin

Xanadu (Utah)   Xanthia (S.Africa) Xa An (Vietnam)

Yukon   Yugoslavia   Yalta

Zaire   Zambia   Zimbabwe

VERBS PRESENT (Tense)
I talk. She talks.

CAPITAL
S

Verbs show action.   **talk**
Verbs show tense.   **I talk.** (present tense = now)
Verbs agree with subjects. **I talk. She talks.**

Cursive   Print   Start on the dot.

𝒮   ʿS   · S   · S

☐ Write & Check

Copy **She**. Make the verbs agree by adding **-s**. End with a period.

I talk.   She talks.

I listen.

I smile.

I grin.

I wonder.

Pick names that start with **S** and write sentences. Make the verbs agree.
Add **-es** because the verbs end in **sh**, **ch**, or **x**. End with a period.

We watch.   Sarah watches.

We fax.

We fix.

We rush.

We stretch.

The FINE Print When the teacher calls the roll, you raise your hand and say, "Present." Present means you're here right now.
In grammar, tense means time. Present tense means the time right now. In present tense, the verbs agree with the subjects.

VERBS PRESENT (Tense)
You <u>surf</u>. He <u>surfs</u>.

Verbs show action. **surf**
Verbs show tense. **You surf.** (present tense = now)
Verbs agree with subjects. **You surf. Henry surfs.**

Cursive   Print   Start on the dot.

H   H   H   H   ☐ Write & Check **H**

Copy.

Hawaii   Honolulu   Hula Hoop

_____   _____   _____

Change **I** or **You** to a name that starts with **H**. Make the verbs agree. Add **-s**. End with a period.

I surf. _____   Henry surfs. _____

I swim. _____   _____

You float. _____   _____

You wear a lei. _____   _____

Change **I** or **You** to a name that starts with **H**. Make the verbs agree. Add **-es** because the verbs end in **o**, **ch**, or **sh**.
End with a period.

I do the hula. _____   Hanna does the hula. _____

I watch me. _____   _____

You fish. _____   _____

You catch fish. _____   _____

Write sentences about what Hanna and Henry do in Hawaii.

VERBS PAST (Tense)
I <u>danced.</u>

CAPITAL
I

Verbs show action. **dance**
Verbs show tense. **I danced.** (past tense = It already happened.)
Regular verbs add **-d** or **-ed** to make the past tense.

Cursive   Print   Start on the dot.

☐ Write & Check

Change these sentences to past tense.
Add **-ed**.

I report.   I talk.   I wait.

I reported.

For **e** endings, add **-d**.

I vote.   I skate.   I dance.

Change **y** endings to **i**, and add **-ed**.

I carry.   I hurry.   I try.

Double the last letter for vowel-consonant endings, then add **-ed**.

I snap.   I bat.   I skip.

<table>
<tr><td colspan="2">**Is it a duck?**
The 🦆 Test</td></tr>
<tr><td>Looks like a duck?</td><td>Y</td></tr>
<tr><td>Swims like a duck?</td><td>Y</td></tr>
<tr><td>Quacks like a duck?</td><td>Y</td></tr>
<tr><td>It's a duck!</td><td></td></tr>
</table>

Is it a verb?
The VERB Test
Does it work with "to" in front? Yes, it's a verb!

to walk?	Y	to write?	___
to hair?	N	to door?	___
to run?	___	to read?	___
to elephant?	___	to window?	___

VERBS FUTURE (Tense)

She __will skate__.

Verbs show action. **skate**
Verbs show tense. **She will skate.** (Future tense = It will happen, but it hasn't happened yet.)
All verbs use the helping verb **will** to make the future tense.

VERB   WILL + VERB = FUTURE

Write sentences with future tense verbs.

skate   Nina will skate.

run   _____

walk   _____

call   _____

CONTRACTIONS – APOSTROPHES

A contraction is a short form of two words.
An apostrophe substitutes for missing letters.

CONTRACTIONS			
I will	**I'll**	it will	**it'll**
you will	**you'll**	we will	**we'll**
he will	**he'll**	they will	**they'll**
she will	**she'll**	will not	**won't**

FUTURE WITH CONTRACTIONS

Change the words into contractions. Write below.

I will   you will   he will   she will

I'll   _____   _____   _____

it will   we will   they will   will not

_____   _____   _____   _____

Write a sentence about something you hope will happen in the future.

_____

_____

The FINE Print   When grammar teachers say "tense," they're not talking about tense muscles or being uptight. They're talking about verbs.
   Present tense means now.
   Past   tense means it already happened.
   Future tense means it will happen.

CAPITALS
C O Q G A T J

Cursive	Print	Start on the dot.		
C	C	C	C	C	☐ Write & Check
O	O	O	O	O	☐ Write & Check
2	Q	Q	Q	Q	☐ Write & Check
G	G	G	G	G	☐ Write & Check
a	A	A	A	A	☐ Write & Check
J	T	T	T	T	☐ Write & Check
J	J	J	J	J	☐ Write & Check

Change cursive to print. Rewrite these capital letters in print.

C   O   2   G   a   J   J

40 *Can-Do Print*

© 2013 Handwriting Without Tears

CAPITALIZATION RULES

Copy each capital next to the example.

A	B	C	D	E	F	G
H	I	J	K	L	M	N
O	P	Q	R	S	T	U
V	W	X	Y	Z		

CAPITALIZATION RULES

Always capitalize the first word in a sentence and the pronoun **I**. Here are some other capitalization rules.

Capitalize: Complete the sentences.

Name of a person   My name is _____.

Initials   My initials are _____.

Days   Today is _____.

Months   My birthday is in _____.

Holidays   My favorite holiday is _____.

Languages   I speak _____.

Titles and names   My teachers name is _____.

Schools   My school is _____.

First, last, and important words in book titles   My favorite book is _____.

First word of a quotation   My friend said, " _____ "

Cities, towns, states, and provinces   I live in _____.

Rivers, lakes, and oceans   The closest water is _____.

Write sentences about places you would like to visit. Using the capitalization rules above, see how many capitals you can include.

ADJECTIVES

happy, cheerful
hairy, bald

Adjectives describe nouns.
Adjectives tell how many, what kind, color, or condition.

SYNONYMS
Synonyms are words that mean the same or nearly the same.
See the synonym pairs below.

Synonyms   **Synonyms**

Copy below the models.

happy   cheerful   angry   furious
_____   _____

elderly   old   large   huge
_____   _____

ANTONYMS
Antonyms are words that have the opposite, or nearly the opposite meaning. Here are some "hairy" antonyms. See the antonym pairs below.

Antonyms   **Antonyms**

Change cursive to print. Rewrite the cursive adjectives in print.

hairy   bald   long   short
_____   _____

thick   thin   frizzy   straight
_____   _____

Draw hair.

© 2013 Handwriting Without Tears

ADJECTIVES

Some adjectives describe just one thing. **cold** day
Comparative adjectives compare two things. **colder** day
Superlative adjectives compare three or more things. **coldest** day

ADJECTIVE	COMPARATIVE -er Write the comparative forms. Add **-er**.	SUPERLATIVE -est Write the comparative forms. Add **-est**.
cold	colder	coldest
few		
dark		
neat		

Change the **y** to **i** first.

friendly	friendlier	friendliest
messy		
sunny		
happy		

ADJECTIVE	"more" COMPARATIVE Write the comparative forms. Add **more**.	"most" SUPERLATIVE Write the comparative forms. Add **most**.
modern	more modern	most modern
stylish		
useful		
careful		

PRONOUNS - SUBJECT CASE

1ˢᵗ, 2ⁿᵈ, 3ʳᵈ Person

Pronouns take the place of nouns.

Subject pronouns take the place of subject nouns.

Joe is drinking a milkshake.

He is drinking a milkshake.

PERSON	SINGULAR - 1	PLURAL 2 or mor
First	I	we
Second	you	you
Third	he, she, it	they

HEY! *I* AM THE FIRST PERSON.

YOU ARE THE SECOND PERSON.

HE IS THE THIRD PERSON.

The FINE Print   **Singular** nouns and pronouns name one. **boy/he**
Plural nouns and pronouns name two or more. **kids/they**
When teachers talk about **number**, they mean singular or plural.
When teachers talk about **person**, they mean first person, second person, or third person.
When teachers talk about **gender**, they mean masculine or feminine. **he/she**

PRONOUNS - OBJECT CASE

me, you, him, her, it
us, you, them

Object pronouns take the place of object nouns.
>She called **Joe**.
>She called **him**.

The subject pronoun does the action. **She**
The verb shows action. She **called**
The object pronoun receives the action. She called **him.**

SUBJECT PRONOUN → **VERB** → **OBJECT PRONOUN**

She and he → called → us.

SUBJECT PRONOUNS	VERBS	OBJECT PRONOUNS
I, you, he, she, we, they, he and I, she and I, he and she, you and I, you and he	asked, called, found, saw, praised, visited, called	me, you, him, her, us, them, him and her, her and him, you and me, you and her

Write your own sentences in **subject → verb → object** order.
Choose the subject pronouns, verbs, and object pronouns from the groups above.

1. _____

2. _____

3. _____

4. _____

5. _____

6. _____

7. _____

The FINE Print   Choose the pronoun by the job it does in the sentence.
   If a pronoun is the **subject** of the sentence, use a **subject pronoun**.
   If a pronoun is the **object** of a verb or preposition, use an **object pronoun**.

PRONOUNS - POSSESSIVE CASE

my, your, his, her, our, your, their

Possessive pronouns show ownership.
They take the place of possessive nouns.

Patrick's car
his car

Meagan's car
her car

the car's trunk
its trunk

Mike and Greg's mom
their mom

Give these possessive pronouns something to own by filling in the blanks. Choose from the cursive list below and rewrite in p

shoes	bike	party	friends	shirt	pizza	soda	money	present

my _____   your_____   his_____   her_____

its _____   our_____   your_____   their_____

These possessive pronouns show ownership. Fill in the blanks. Choose from the cursive pronouns and rewrite in print.

mine	yours	his	hers	ours	theirs

This bus is _____, but that bus is _____.

This book is _____, but that book is _____.

This pizza is _____, but the calzone is _____.

This bike is _____, but that bike is _____.

Three Little Kittens

Do you remember "Three Little Kittens"? Not only did they lose their mittens; they also lost their pronouns. Help Mother Goose get this rhyme right!

Fill in the missing pronouns. Choose the correct cursive pronouns from the list below and rewrite in print.

we	you	they	our	your	their

Three little kittens, _____ lost their mittens,

And _____ began to cry, Oh, Mother Dear, _____ sadly fear,

_____ mittens _____ have lost. What! Lost _____ mittens!

_____ naughty kittens! Then _____ shall have no pie.

The FINE Print   Choosing the right pronoun is easy as pie if you know the job it does in the sentence. (**Whose** is also a possessive case pronoun.)

PRONOUN REVIEW

You've heard of suitcases, briefcases, and guitar cases.
The pronoun plane has landed. Here are the pronoun cases.

SUBJECT PRONOUN CASE

A **subject** case pronoun tells who the sentence is about: **I** get the case.

I	**we**
you	**you**
he, she, it	**they**

OBJECT PRONOUN CASE

An **object** case pronoun is the object of a verb: You watch **me**.

or

An **object** case pronoun is the object of a preposition.   This case is for **me**.

me	**us**
you	**you**
him, her, it	**them**

POSSESSIVE PRONOUN CASE

A **possessive case** pronoun owns something.   Is it **yours** or **mine**?
It's **my** case.

my, mine	**our, ours**
your, yours	**you, yours**
his, her, hers, its	**their, theirs**

NOUNS –SINGULAR POSSESSIVE

Singular means one. To make singular nouns possessive, just add **'s**.

SINGLE PEOPLE
1. Make a list of 8 people.
2. Start each name with a capital. **Luis**
3. Add **'s**. **Luis's**
4. Give each person a possession. **Luis's gerbil**

1. Luis's gerbil _____   5. _____

2. _____   6. _____

3. _____   7. _____

4. _____   8. _____

Articles **a** or **an** go before singular nouns.
Use **a** before nouns that start with a consonant sound. **a bird, a cat**
Use **an** before nouns that start with a vowel sound. **an ant, an eagle**

SINGLE ANIMALS
1. Make a list of 8 animals down the middle column.
2. Write **a** or **an** before each animal. **an elephant**
3. Add **'s**. **an elephant's**
4. Give each animal a possession. **an elephant's trunk**

Draw one of the animals.

1. an   elephant's   trunk

2. _____ _____ _____

3. _____ _____ _____

4. _____ _____ _____

5. _____ _____ _____

6. _____ _____ _____

7. _____ _____ _____

8. _____ _____ _____

The FINE Print   **The** is a definite article. Use **the** before specific nouns. Use **the** before singular or plural nouns: **the** boy, **the** boys.

NOUNS - PLURAL POSSESSIVE   Add ' or 's

There are two ways to make plural nouns possessive.
1. Add **'s** to nouns that do not end in **s**.   **men → men's**
2. Add **'** to nouns that end in **s**.   **ladies → ladies'**

COLUMN 1 Copy the nouns that **do not end in s**: Add **'s**	PLURAL NOUNS	COLUMN 2 Copy the nouns that **end in s**: Add **'**
women's	women	
	citizens	citizens'
	men	
	friends	
	kids	
	cattle	
	cows	
	children	
	ushers	
	cars	
	buses	
	geese	
	ladies	
	states	
	cities	

IRREGULAR VERBS

There are regular verbs and irregular verbs.
Regular verbs add **-d** or **-ed** to talk about the past.
I **walk**.   I **walked**.   I have **walked**.

Irregular verbs are rule breakers. They have their own forms.
I **give**.   I **gave**.   I have **given**.

Here is a list of some irregular verbs.

PRESENT	PAST	(have, has, had) + PAST PARTICIPLE
break	broke	broken
choose	chose	chosen
do	did	done
eat	ate	eaten
go	went	gone
give	gave	given
hide	hid	hidden
know	knew	known
leave	left	left
take	took	taken

have
has   +
had

Past participles are verb forms that use a helping "have" verb.

Fill in the missing forms for each verb. Use the chart above if you need help.

	PRESENT	PAST	(have, has, or had) + PAST PARTICIPLE
1.	break	broke	have broken
2.	know		have
3.	do		have
4.	take		have
5.	choose		has
6.	go		has
7.	hide		has
8.	give		had
9.	leave		had
10.	eat		had

The FINE Print   Inside story: **ir** = not. **Ir**regular verbs are not regular. Look up irregular verbs in a dictionary to find their past tense and past participle forms. Many grammar books have irregular verb charts.

HELPING "have" VERBS

Have, **has**, **had** are helping "**have**" verbs.
A helping **have** verb + past participle = perfect verb tense.
Perfect verb tenses can happen in the present, in the past, and in the future.

PRESENT PERFECT
have (or has) + past particple

Copy below the models.

We have walked for miles.

They have taken a break.

> HEY, WHAT MAKES THEM PERFECT?

Copy.

He has eaten lunch.   She has left town.

PAST PERFECT
had + past participle

Copy.

Joe had bought two tickets.

FUTURE PERFECT
will have + past participle

Copy.

I will have finished by noon.

☐ Check Sentence

The FINE Print   What makes a perfect tense? The words **have, has, had** tell you it's a perfect tense.
"Perfect" usually has a different meaning. This is just the "English grammar" use of the word "perfect."

LINKING VERBS

LINKING "be" VERBS
Linking "be" verbs don't act; they don't even help other verbs.
Linking verbs work alone. They make a statement or tell it like it is: **Dr. Less is nice.**

LINKING "sensory" VERBS
Linking "sensory" verbs tell how things look, feel, sound, taste, or smell. They link the sentence together.
He **looks** happy. I **feel** bad. It **sounds** great. My burrito **tastes** good. Your socks **smell** awful.

SUBJECT	→	LINKING VERB	→	WORD OR PHRASE (ADJECTIVE)

Make up sentences using linking verbs. Don't forget the punctuation.

1. The burrito → tastes → good.

2. _____ are _____

3. _____ seems _____

4. _____ is _____

5. _____ looks _____

6. _____ sounds _____

Write about your favorite food. What does it look like? How does it taste? What is the smell?

HELPING "be" VERBS

The "**be**" verbs aren't just linking verbs. They can also be helping verbs.
The helping "**be**" verbs include **am**, **is**, **are**, **was**, **were**, **will be**, **has been**.
Present participles are the **ing** form of the verb. **eat** → **eating**
Helping "**be**" verbs and present participles work together. I **am eating**. I **was eating**. I **will be eating**.

PRESENT PARTICIPLES = PLAIN VERB + ing

Write present participles.

eat + ing   = _____   wait + ing   = _____

cook + ing   = _____   paint + ing   = _____

talk + ing   = _____   sail + ing   = _____

CONTRACTIONS & APOSTROPHES

Remember contractions? They're short forms of two words. Letters
are left out. An apostrophe takes the place of the missing letters.

CONTRACTIONS	
I am	**I'm**
you are	**you're**
she is	**she's**
he is	**he's**
it is	**it's**
we are	**we're**
you are	**you're**
they are	**they're**

Change cursive to print. Rewrite these cursive sentences with contractions.
Use print.

I am thinking.   I'm thinking.

You are cooking.   _____

She is talking.   _____

He is waiting.   _____

It is raining.   _____

We are performing.   _____

You are singing.   _____

They are screaming.   _____

☐ Check Sentence

ADVERBS

Adverbs tell when, how often, where, why, and how.

Adverbs usually describe verbs.   The dog **never** bites.
Adverbs sometimes describe other adverbs. She barked **very** loudly.
Adverbs occasionally describe adjectives. She's a **really** good dog.

HOW OFTEN?

| never | rarely | sometimes | usually | always |

These adverbs tell how often, from never to always.

Answer these questions with complete sentences. Choose from the adverbs above. Stop with a period.

Change cursive to print.

How often do you
. . . eat chicken?   I sometimes eat chicken.
. . . drink milk?   I
. . . make your bed?   I
. . . do the dishes?   I
. . . read the comics?   I
. . . go fishing?   I
. . . read mysteries?   I

Write about your everyday life. What do you always do? What do you never do?

_____

_____

_____

_____

ADVERBS

Adverbs tell how someone acts or does something.
Many adverbs end in **-ly**.

ANTONYMS

An antonym is a word that means the opposite.
Here are pairs of antonyms that are adverbs.

Antonyms

Copy one word of each pair. It's your choice.

bravely	fearfully
deliberately	accidentally
loudly	quietly
roughly	tenderly

Antonyms

carefully	carelessly
formally	informally
quickly	slowly
well	poorly

Adverbs tell how someone does something.
Do you play a sport or musical instrument? Write about something you do using an adverb that ends in **-ly**.

The FINE Print   Not all words that end in **-ly** are adverbs. Friendly, ugly, costly, and others are adjectives. Check a dictionary.

PREPOSITIONS

Prepositions show position or time.
Copy the prepositions below the models.

above	before	up	over	in
below	after	down	under	out
during	inside	on	between	around
since	outside	off	beside	through

GOING ON A PREPOSITION HUNT

Go on a bear hunt and a preposition hunt. Underline the prepositions you find in "Going on a Bear Hunt."
Use the list above for clues.

GOING ON A BEAR HUNT

We're going on a bear hunt,
We're gonna catch a big one,
I'm not afraid! Are you? Not me!

I see tall grass,
Can't go over it,
Let's go through it.

I see a bridge,
Can't go around it,
Let's go over it.

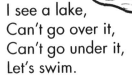

I see a lake,
Can't go over it,
Can't go under it,
Let's swim.

I see a tree,
Can't go over it,
Can't go under it,
Let's go up it,
I don't see any bears,
Let's go down.

I see a swamp,
Can't go over it,
Can't go under it,
Let's go through it.

I see a cave,
Can't go over it,
Can't go under it,
Let's go in.
I see two eyes, I see two ears,
I see a nose, I see a mouth,
Yikes! It's a bear!
Let's get out of here.

PREPOSITIONAL PHRASES

over the rainbow

Over the rainbow is not a sentence.
Over the rainbow is a phrase.
Over the rainbow starts with a preposition.
Over the rainbow is a prepositional phrase.

A phrase is a group of related words.
A phrase has a subject or a verb, but not both.
Prepositional phrases start with a preposition.
Make up prepositional phrases.
Add an article (**a**, **an**, or **the**) and a noun.

PREPOSITION	ARTICLE	NOUN
over	the	rainbow
under		
behind		
during		
beside		
on		
into		
inside		
around		

PREPOSITIONAL PHRASES IN SENTENCES

Change cursive to print. Rewrite these cursive sentences in print.

My hamster ran under the bed.

After the game, we raced home.

☐ Check Sentence

The FINE Print   **After the game** is an introductory phrase. Use a comma after an introductory phrase.

CONJUNCTIONS

Conjunctions are words that join words, phrases, or clauses.

COMPOUND SENTENCES

Two sentences joined = one compound sentence.
There are two ways to make compound sentences:
    1. Use a comma and a conjunction. **, and**   **, or**   **, but**
    2. Use a semicolon. **;**

COMMA and CONJUNCTION

,and
, or
, but

Let's get ready to write compound sentences with commas and conjunctions.

Copy the commas and conjunctions below the models:

, and   , or   , but   , so   , yet   , for   , nor

Use a comma and a conjuction to join the sentences. See the example below.

    Mr. Wright has a new car.   Mr. Case has an old car.
    Mr. Wright has a new car**,** **but** Mr. Case has an old car.

comma, conjunction

The boys can stay.   They must leave soon.

Ann sings.   Tom plays the piano.

SEMICOLON ;

Use a semicolon to join the sentences. See the example below.

    Dr. Less writes books. Her friend illustrates them.
    Dr. Less writes books**;** her friend illustrates them.

semicolon   lowercase h

We went to Ohio.   They went to Alberta.

The FINE Print   The root **semi** = half, so a semicolon **(;)** is half a colon **(:)**. Use semicolons to link related ideas.

ABBREVIATIONS

Abreviations are shortened words. Use a period after an abbreviation. **Doctor → Dr.**

TITLES
Change cursive to print. Change these abbreviations to print.

Dr.   Mr.   Mrs.   Ms.

ABBREVIATE THE DAYS
Abbreviate the days of the week. Find the answers upside down.

Monday   Tuesday   Wednesday   Thursday

Friday   Saturday   Sunday

Mon. Tue. Wed. Thur. Fri. Sat. Sun.

MONTHS
May, June, and July are short. They are not abbreviated and do not use periods. Change cursive to print.
Rewrite these cursive abbreviations in print.

Jan.   Feb.   Mar.   Apr.

Aug.   Sept.   Oct.   Nov.   Dec.

ABBREVIATE THE WORDS
Change these words to abbreviations.

Doctor   Monday   March   December   August

PUNCTUATION

Look at all the places a comma should be.
- In a series
- After an introductory clause
- Before conjunctions used to separate clauses
- Before quoting a speaker
- Between a city and a state
- In a date, between the day and the year

Copy below the models. Don't forget any commas!

Commas – in a series

keys, socket wrench, screwdriver, pump

Commas – after an introductory clause

When he finished the course,

Comma – before conjunctions used to separate clauses

He wants a new bike, but he can't afford one.

Comma – before quoting a speaker

Scottie said,   Rachelle said,

Comma – between a city and a state

Tulsa, Oklahoma   Baltimore, Maryland

Commas – in dates, between the day and the year

Sept. 1, 2013   Oct. 31, 2013

QUOTATIONS

Quotation marks show someone's exact words.
Learn to write quotations from the comics. Here are two styles to try.

TWO WAYS TO WRITE QUOTATIONS

1 - The NAME comes first.
Mr. Case said, "My car is a lemon."

2 - The QUOTE comes first.
"My car is a lemon," said Mr. Case.

Diver Dave said, "I love to dive."

or

"I love to dive,"
said Diver Dave.

Racing Robin yelled, "Go, go, go!"

or

"Go, go, go!" yelled Racing Robin.

Cadago asked, "Do you need help?"

or

"Do you need help?" asked Cadago.

Your choice. Copy some of the quotations above, or copy a quotation from your favorite comic strip.

_____

_____

_____

Make up a comic strip. Draw characters and give them quote bubbles. Fill in the bubbles with what the characters say.
Use a blank sheet of paper.

INTERJECTIONS!

Interjections are not sentences. Interjections are just one or two words that express feelings.

1. Strong interjections end with an exclamation point.
   Yikes!   Rats!   Whew!   Gosh!   Good grief!

2. A comma follows mild interjections.
   Hey, I'm next.   **Oh**, I understand.   **Well**, that's over.   **Hmm**, let's go.

HEY, WHAT'S WITH THE TOGA?

Make up some interjections for these situations. Write your interjections in print.

The doctor just gave you a shot. _____

Someone just cut ahead of you in line. _____

You won the bike race. _____

You came in last. _____

The pool water is ice cold. _____

Friends surprise you with a big cake. _____

PRINTING WITH GREEK & LATIN

In the ancient world, Greek and Latin were widely spoken.
The Romans spoke Latin. People in Greece spoke Greek. They still do.
This magnified (**magn** = big) view shows Greece and Italy (and Rome).

THIS IS A HEMISPHERE.
HEMI = HALF
SPHERE = GLOBE, BALL

HEY, IT'S EASY!

More than 60 percent of English words come from Greek and Latin. Knowing a little Greek and Latin
is like knowing a secret code. You have an easy way to figure out words.

GREEK & LATIN Copy.		MEANING	ENGLISH WORDS
port	=	carry	export, portable, deport, portfolio, porter
micro	=	small	microscope, microwave, microchip, microbe
ology	=	study of	psychology, biology, zoology, sociology, anthropology

capital →

column →

The FINE Print   A column is a tall pillar that supports a building or a statue. The top of a column is called a capital.

GETTING TO THE ROOT OF THINGS

PREFIXES come first—**pre**view, **re**turn. Copy the prefixes.

pre _____   re _____

_____ = before   _____ = again

ROOTS are main word parts—**aqua**tic, tri**cycle**. Copy the roots.

aqua _____   cycl _____

_____ = water   _____ = circle, wheel

SUFFIXES come after roots—aqu**arium**, solid**ify**. Copy the suffixes.

arium _____   ify _____

_____ = place for   _____ = to make

BUILDING WORDS WITH PREFIXES

The prefix pre = before.

Copy pre.   Combine the parts to make a new word.

(pre) + dict = predict _____

(_____) + pare = _____

(_____) + vent = _____

The prefix re = again.

Copy re.   Combine the parts to make a new word.

(re) + form = _____

(_____) + fund = _____

(_____) + read = _____

The FINE Print   There are three styles of Greek capitals. The capitals at the top of this page are Ionic capitals. They look like a scroll.

GROWING WORDS

GROWING WORDS WITH ROOTS

The root <u>port</u> = carry.

Copy <u>port</u>.

Combine the parts to make a new word.

trans + (port) = transport

ex + (_____) = _____

(_____) + folio = _____

(_____) + able = _____

The root <u>scope</u> = look at.

Copy <u>scope</u>.

Combine the parts to make a new word.

tele + (scope) = _____

peri + (_____) = _____

kaleido + (_____) = _____

BUILDING WORDS WITH SUFFIXES

The suffix <u>meter</u> = measure.

Copy <u>meter</u>.

Combine the parts to make a new word.

thermo + (meter) = _____

peri + (_____) = _____

baro + (_____) = _____

The suffix <u>ify</u> = to make.

Copy <u>ify</u>.

Combine the parts to make a new word.

solid + (ify) = _____

liqu + (_____) = _____

ampl + (_____) = _____

The FINE Print   The capitals on this page are Corinthian capitals. They have leaves.

WORD DETECTIVES

GREEK ROOTS

Change these roots from *cursive* to print.

sphere _____   meter _____   therm _____   magn _____

_____   _____   _____   _____

GUESSING GREEK

Look at the root and the clue words that use the root. Then guess what the root means. Find the answers upside down.

<u>sphere</u> – hemisphere, spherical, atmosphere, stratosphere

I guess sphere means _____

<u>meter</u> – speedometer, barometer, thermometer, diameter

I guess meter means _____

<u>therm</u> – thermal, thermos, thermometer, thermostat

I guess therm means _____

<u>magn</u> – magnify, magnificent, magnanimous, magnification

I guess magn means _____

sphere = ball, meter = measure, therm = heat, magn = large

Draw a picture of the underlined word and then write the definition:

A <u>magnifying glass</u> is _____

_____

A <u>thermometer</u> is _____

_____

The FINE Print   The capitals on this page are Doric capitals.

LXVI 66 *Can-Do Print*   © 2013 Handwriting Without Tea

WORD DETECTIVES

Here are more familiar Greek and Latin roots:

astro
stella
> = star

naut = sailor

con = together

octo = eight

cycl = wheel, circle

photo = light

graph = write, draw

ped
pod
> = foot

micro = small

scope = look at

tri = three

Decode the words below by writing the meaning of their roots. Write your answers in print.

tricycle   = ___three___   + ___wheels___

microscope   = _____   + _____

astronaut   = _____   + _____

photograph   = _____   + _____

tripod   = _____   + _____

constellation   = _____   + _____

(Tip: The suffix **-tion** = state of, condition)

Now draw pictures of some of the things listed on the page.

Greek and Latin help you decipher big science words:

ornithology	biology	paleontology	geology	zoology	entomology

bio = life   entomon = insect   ology = study of

ge = earth   ornith = bird   ologist = one who studies

mar = sea   zo = animal

paleo = old

Choose from the following list to match the scientists to what they study. Write your answers in print.

biologist	entomologist	geologist	~~marine biologist~~	ornithologist	paleontologist	zoologist

marine biologist _____   sea life

_____   birds

_____   insects

_____   structure of the earth

_____   living things

_____   old life forms and fossils

_____   animals

DID YOU SEE THAT ORNITHOLOGIST WATCHING US?

The FINE Print   The suffix **-ist** = an expert in. Do you know any other **-ist** experts? What about an anthropologist, a scientist, or an astrophysicist?

LXVIII **68** *Can-Do Print*

© 2013 Handwriting Without Tears

SIZE SCIENCE

Knowing roots helps you make smart guesses about words.
Dig into the root micro.

microscope   **micro**wave   **micro**meter

What does micro mean? _____

What is a micrometer? Take a guess.

___small bug   ___device for small measurements   ___small parking meter

Guess what these things are. Write your guesses in print. Find the answers upside down.

microcomputer   =   _____

microscope   =   _____

microwave   =   _____

micrometer = device for making small measurements, microcomputer = small computer, microscope = instrument to see small things, microwave = small electromagnetic wave used in cooking

THINK BIG!

magn = great, big, large   opus = work   charta = document

Complete these sentences. Choose from the words below. The roots will help you. Remember your periods.

| magnify | magnificent | magnitude | Magna Carta | magnum opus |

To make larger is to _____

England's 1215 document is the _____

Something impressive or beautiful is _____

The size or importance of something is the _____

A great, often artistic work is a _____

The FINE Print   Magna Carta is also written Magna Charta. Magnet and magnolia come from different roots, not **magn** = big.

THE NUMBER STORY

I	1	uni – unicycle, uniform, unit
II	2	bi – bicycle, biceps, bilingual
III	3	tri – tricycle, triple, triangle, triatholon
IV	4	quad, tetra – quadriceps, quadruplets, tetrology
V	5	quin, penta – quintuplets, quintet, pentagon, pentathlon
VI	6	sex, hex – sextet, hexagon
VII	7	sept – septagon
VIII	8	oct, octo – octopus, octagon, octave
IX	9	novem
X	10	dec, decem, deca – decade, decimal
L	50	quinquaginta
C	100	cent – century, centennial, cent

Finish the sentences. Find clues above. Find the answers upside down.

II ___ A bicycle has _____

III ___ A tricycle has _____

V ___ The pentagon has _____

C ___ A century has _____

two wheels, three wheels, five sides, 100 years

Change these roots from cursive to print. They help with metric words.

deci
_____ = tenth

centi
_____ = hundredth

milli
_____ = thousandth

meter
_____ = unit of measure

Change these metric words from cursive to print.

decimeter

centimeter

millimeter

1/10th of a meter

1/100th of a meter

1/1000th of a meter

The FINE Print   With September our ninth month, you'd think that **sept** meant nine. It doesn't. On the Roman calendar, September was the 7th month; October the 8th; November the 9th; and December the 10th month. We use a different calendar now.

© 2013 Handwriting Without Tear

MATH WORDS MADE EASY!

Friends, Romans, countrymen, step right up for the inside story on math words.
Know the roots. PRESTO! Know the meanings.

angul	} = angle	
gon		
hex	= 6	
iso	= equal	
oct	= 8	
parallelos	= parallel	
penta	= 5	
poly	= many	
rect	= right	
tri	= three	

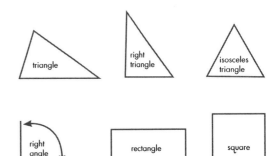

TRIANGLES have 3 sides and 3 angles.

Copy these roots and meanings.

tri = 3   gon = angle   iso = equal   rect = right

Copy.

triangle △   right triangle ◣   isosceles triangle △

RECTANGLES have 4 sides and 4 right angles.
SQUARES have 4 equal sides and 4 right angles.

Copy.

rect = right   rectangles   square ☐

OTHER SHAPES

Write the number of sides beside each shape. Copy the words.

pentagon = _5_   hexagon = ____   octagon = ____   triangle = ____

The FINE Print   Rect = right. Right angles are corner angles, like the corner of this page or a printed **L**.

HEAD TO TOE

GREEK

cephal = head
rhino = nose
odont = tooth
stetho = chest
derm = skin
dactyl = finger, toe
pod = foot

LATIN

capit = head
cardi = heart
dent = tooth
pulmon = lung
manu = hand
digit = finger, toe
ped = foot

BONUS ROOT ortho = straight (He's standing straight and he's got straight teeth!)

Change these English words that are based on Greek or Latin roots from cursive to print.

rhinoceros

manual

digital

dentures

pedestrian

stethoscope

Change cursive to print. Rewrite these doctors in print.

dermatologist   podiatrist   cardiologist   orthodontist

What body part do the doctors take care of? Fill in the blanks and end each sentence with a period.

A dermatologist takes care of the _____

A podiatrist takes care of the _____

A cardiologist takes care of the _____

An orthodontist straightens the _____

The FINE Print Many medical and scientific terms come from these roots. Ask your parents about these and other medical specialists. A pediatrician takes care of children, not feet! Podiatrists take care of feet.

SOUNDS ALL AROUND

Check out these clues:

audio = hear, hearing

audit = hear, hearing

caco = bad

eu = good

mega = big

meter = device for measuring

micro = small

orium = place for

phon = sound

tele = far

WHAT IS IT?

Fill in the blanks with one of the print answers below.

telephone	cacophony	audit orium	phonics

A big place to see and hear performances: _____

A sound that's awful, harsh, and off-key: _____

It rings: _____

Letter and word sounds: _____

microphone	megaphone	euphonious	audio meter

A device for measuring hearing: _____

Pleasant-sounding to the ear: _____

Singers hold me: _____

Cheerleaders use it to make their voices loud: _____

Write a sentence with one of these sound words.

_____

_____

VAST SEAS

Sail the seas with Greek and Latin roots.

Change *cursive* to print. Rewrite these cursive roots in print.

aqua = water

aqua

hydro = water

_____

fire **hydra**nt

nav = ship

_____

sub = under

_____

mar = sea

_____

endo = inner

_____

exo = outer

_____

skeleto = skeleton

_____

peri = around

_____

scope = look at

_____

Fill in the blanks. Choose the correct cursive answer and rewrite in print.

| periscope | submarine | exoskeleton | endoskeleton | navy | marine |

Look through the _____ on our yellow _____!

I'm a lobster. I have an _____.

I'm a shark. I have an _____.

A sailor has enlisted in the _____.

I work on coral reefs. I'm studying _____ life.

Write a watery sentence or two.

_____

_____

The night sky is filled with stars. Constellations are groups of stars.

con = together   **stella** = star   **canis** = dog   **ursa** = bear   **major** = big

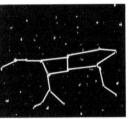

Ursa Major = The Big Bear

Copy these sentences.

The Big Dipper is part of Ursa Major.

_____

Sirius is the brightest star.

_____

Canis Major = The Big Dog

Sirius is part of Canis Major.

PLANETS

A mnemonic helps you remember something. Use this mnemonic for the order of the planets:

"**M**y   **V**ery   **E**xcellent   **M**other   **J**ust   **S**erved   **U**s   **N**oodles!"

Write the planet names in order from the sun.

Earth	Jupiter	Mars	Mercury	Neptune	Saturn	Uranus	Venus

Mercury	J
V	S
E	U
M	N

The FINE Print   Cool roots: **astro** = star, **naut** = sailor. Cool meaning: Astronauts are star sailors! Think of S.U.N. to remember the three planets that are the farthest from the sun.

You walk on terra firma.

In Latin, **terra** = earth, land
firma = solid

Change cursive to print. Rewrite these cursive earth words in print.

territory

terrarium

terrain

geography

geology

geoscience

Botany is the study of plants. Some botany roots:

chloro = green	**hydro** = water	**stella** = star
epi = on, upon	**ology** = study of	**trop** = turn
ge = earth	**phyll** = leaf	**zo** = animal
helio = sun	**phyt** = plant	

Write the meanings of the roots in print. See how the root meanings compare with the actual definition.

WORD	ROOT MEANINGS		ACTUAL DEFINITION
chlorophyll =	green	+ leaf	A green substance in plants
epiphyte =		+	A plant that grows on other plants
geology =		+	The study of Earth's soil and rock layers
hydrology =		+	The study of water
heliotropic =		+	Turning toward the sun
zoology =		+	Study of animals
stellaria =			Small white flowers shaped like stars

Did you ever do a science project about plants?
Describe your project.

The FINE Print   Here's a great word: **zoophyte**. What could an "animal plant" be? Zoophytes are animals that look like plants—sea anemones, corals, and sponges, for instance. (They're invertebrates—no backbone: **in** = not + **vertebra** = joint.)

FALSE CLUES : "TRI" AGAIN!

Sometimes you'll spot what looks like a Greek or Latin clue, but it won't be a true clue. Take **tri,** for example. Don't be tricked. Not all words with **tri** are related to the root **tri,** meaning three.

These words **are NOT related to the prefix tri.**

Change cursive to print. Rewrite the cursive words in print.

tribe   trick   trim   trip

tribe _____   _____   _____   _____

These words are **related to the prefix tri.**

Change cursive to print. Rewrite the cursive tri words in print.

triangle   triplicate   tricycle

triangle _____   _____   _____

triceratops   tripod   triplets

_____   _____   _____

trilogy   trident   trio

_____   _____   _____

Draw three pictures of **tri** words.

TRY THIS - TRANSLATE

Grab your togas and laurel wreaths!
Translate these Greek and Latin roots. Print your answers. Find the answers upside down.

	GREEK/LATIN	ENGLISH		GREEK/LATIN	ENGLISH
1.	aqua, hydro	= _____	16.	manu	= _____
2.	astro, stella	= _____	17.	meter	= _____
3.	canis	= _____	18.	micro	= _____
4.	cardi	= _____	19.	milli	= _____
5.	capit, cephal	= _____	20.	octo	= _____
6.	con	= _____	21.	paleo	= _____
7.	dactyl, digit	= _____	22.	ped, pod	= _____
8.	dent	= _____	23.	phon, son	= _____
9.	derm	= _____	24.	phyt	= _____
10.	eu	= _____	25.	poly	= _____
11.	ge	= _____	26.	port	= _____
12.	gon, angul	= _____	27.	pre	= _____
13.	helio	= _____	28.	tele	= _____
14.	iso	= _____	29.	terra	= _____
15.	magn, mega	= _____	30.	trop	= _____

1. water
2. star
3. dog
4. heart
5. head
6. with, together
7. finger, toe
8. tooth
9. skin
10. good
11. earth
12. angle
13. sun
14. equal
15. big
16. hand
17. measure
18. small
19. thousand
20. eight
21. old
22. foot
23. sound
24. plant
25. many
26. carry
27. before
28. far
29. earth, land
30. turn, change

LXXVIII 78 *Can-Do Print*   © 2013 Handwriting Without Tea

A **angul, gon** = angle 71, 78
aqua, hydr, hydro = water 64, 74, 76, 78
arium, orium = place for 64, 73
astro, stella = star 67, 75, 76, 78
audit, audio = hear, hearing 73
B **baro** = pressure 65
bi = two 70
bio = life 68
C **caco** = bad 73
canis = dog 75, 78
capit, cephal = head 72, 78
cent = hundred 70
centi = hundredth 70
cephal, capit = head 72, 78
charta = document 69
chloro = green 76
con = together, with 67, 75, 78
cycl = circle, wheel 64, 67
D **dactyl, digit** = toe, finger 72, 78
dec, decem, deca = ten 70
deci = tenth 70
dent, odon, odont = tooth 72, 78
derm = skin 72, 78
digit, dactyl = toe, finger 72, 78
endo = inner 74
entomon = insect 68
E **epi** = on, upon 76
eu = well, good 73, 78
ex = out of 65
exo = outer 74
firma = solid 76
F **folio, phyll** = sheet, leaf 65, 76
G **ge, terra** = earth, land 68, 76, 78
gon, angul = angle 71, 78
graph = write, draw 67
H **helio** = sun 76, 78
hemi = half 63
hex, sex = six 70, 71
hydr, hydro, aqua = water 64, 74, 76, 78
I **-ify** = to make 64, 65
in = not 76
iso = equal 71, 78
-ist = expert in 68
M **magn, major, mega** = big, great, large 63, 66, 69, 73, 75, 78
manu = hand 72, 78
mar = sea 68, 74
meter = measure, device for measuring, unit of measure 65, 66, 70, 73, 78
micro = small 63, 67, 69, 73, 78
milli = thousandth 70, 78
N **naut** = sailor 67, 75
nav = ship 74
novem = nine 70

O **oct, octo** = eight 67, 70, 71, 78
odon, odont, dent = tooth 72, 78
ologist = one who studies 68
ology = study of 63, 68, 76
opus = work 69
orium, arium = place for 64, 73
ornith = bird 68
ortho = straight 72
P **paleo** = old 68, 78
parallelos = parallel 71
ped, pod = foot 67, 72, 78
penta, quin = five 70, 71
peri = around 65, 74
phyt = plant 76, 76
phon, son = sound 73, 78
photo = light 67
phyll, folio = leaf 65, 76
phyt = plant 76, 78
pod, ped = foot 67, 72, 78
poly = many 71, 78
port = carry 63, 65, 78
pre = before 64, 78
pulmon = lung 72
Q **quad, tetra** = four 70
quin, penta = five 70, 71
quinquaginta = fifty 70
R **re** = again 64
rect = right 71
rhino = nose 72
S **scope** = look at 65, 67, 74
semi = half 58
sept = seven 70
sex, hex = six 70
skeleto = skeleton 74
son, phon = sound 73, 78
sphere (from sphaîra) = ball, globe 63, 66
stella, astro = star 67, 75, 76, 78
stetho = chest 72
sub = under 74
T **tele** = far 65, 73, 78
terra, ge, geo = earth, land 68, 76, 78
tetra, quad = four 70
-tion = state of, condition 67
therm, thermo = heat 65, 66
trans = across 65
tri = three 67, 70, 71, 77
trop = turn 76, 78
U **uni** = one 70
ursa = bear 75
V **vertebra** = joint 76
Z **zo** = animal 68, 76

Wow! What a start on Greek and Latin word roots! You're on your way to becoming great word decoders. Try these: endoderm, pulmonologist, mariner, decade, epidermis, microbiology . . . you get the idea! Keep exploring. You've found the key to figuring out new words.

PRINTING & THE WRITER'S NOTEBOOK

These famous writers welcome you to The Writer's Notebook.
Do you recognize any of them?

Emily Dickinson wrote poetry.
Frederick Douglass wrote an autobiography.
Anne Frank wrote a diary.
William Shakespeare wrote plays.
Mark Twain wrote short stories.

Now you are the writer!
In this section, you will be writing on notebook paper.

Your picture here

DETAILS, DETAILS

SPECIFIC DETAILS

For readers to see what you have in mind, use specific words instead of general words.

Write specific words.

sport	→	baseball	toy	→	
dog	→		flower	→	
lunch	→		bird	→	
insect	→		car	→	

SENSORY DETAILS

Make your writing come alive with sensory details.
Tell what readers would see, hear, smell, taste, or touch.

Choose a setting:
1. Spaceship   2. Circus   3. Beach

Setting:

Describe what your reader will:

See:

Hear:

Smell:

Taste:

Touch:

PARAGRAPHS

Keep your paragraphs organized and structured:
1. Tell your reader what you're going to write about. This becomes the topic sentence.
2. Say it. Give supporting facts, details, and thoughts about your topic sentence.
3. Tell your reader what you said. Restate the idea from the topic sentence using different words.

Plan your paragraph.

My topic is:

Thoughts, facts, or details to include:

Write a draft.

1. Topic sentence:

2. Say it.

3. Restate the topic sentence in different words.

PARAGRAPHS

Now, it's time to write your own paragraph. Make sure you have a topic sentence. Don't forget the supporting facts and details. Finish it by restating the topic. Indent to start.

Write your paragraph.

DIARY OR JOURNAL NOTES

Anne Frank died in a concentration camp during World War II. After her death, her father found and published her diary. A diary is a personal book for daily writing. Usually diaries are private. You can buy a blank book for writing your daily thoughts and experiences.

A journal is also for personal, regular writing. Journals help people remember the details of special times or trips. Teachers often have students write in a journal at school. Journal writing develops your ability to observe, reflect, and write well.

Anne Frank
1929–1945

Write about your life today and about your thoughts.

Today's Date:

Thoughts and experiences:

© 2013 Handwriting Without Tea

AUTOBIOGRAPHY NOTES

If you write about your own life, it's an autobiography. Frederick Douglass wrote passionately about growing up as a slave, secretly learning to read and write, and finally becoming a free man.

To write an autobiography, you need:
1. Yourself
2. Places in your life
3. People in your life
4. Events in your life

Frederick Douglass
1818–1895

Write notes for your autobiography.

1. Yourself:

2. Places in your life:

3. People in your life:

4. Events in your life:

Use these notes to write a one-page autobiography. Use a separate piece of paper.

LETTER WRITING

Friendly letters and notes are organized from top to bottom: Date, Greeting, Body, Closing, and Signature. Each part begins on a new line. Dates are at the top right. Greetings begin at the left margin. The body or message is indented like a paragraph. The closing and signature are centered.

DATES
Fill in the year. Copy the dates.

Jan. 1, 201   Feb. 1, 201   Mar. 1, 201

Apr. 1, 201   May 1, 201   June 1, 201

July 1, 201   Aug. 1, 201   Sept. 1, 201

Oct. 1, 201   Nov. 1, 201   Dec. 1, 201

GREETINGS
Copy.

Dear Aunt Alice,   Mr.   Mrs.   Ms.

CLOSINGS
Copy.

Sincerely,   Thank you,   Yours,   Love,

THANK YOU NOTES

Write a thank you letter. Organize your letter like this.

Date
Month Day, Year

Greeting
Dear _____ ,

Body
Say thank you and tell how much you appreciate the gift or help. Mention what it is or what they did. Add details to make it more personal.

Closing
Sincerely, Thank you, or Love,

Signature

Use a comma:
1. After the day of the month
2. After the greeting
3. After the closing

POETRY

Emily Dickinson
1830–1886

Emily Dickinson wrote poetry. There are many kinds of poems. Some rhyme, some don't. Some have a pattern, some don't. Try different types.

Haiku is a three line, 17-syllable poem of Japanese origin that doesn't rhyme. Haiku paints a picture or expresses a feeling.

School Starts

Pencil sharpened, paper fresh and clean,
Ideas swirl in my mind,
I write.

Beach

The ocean waves crashing,
Seagulls flying high above,
The sand is hot.

Try writing a Haiku.

1st line:

2nd line:

3rd line:

Now, it's time to write a different kind of poem. Pick a favorite person, sport or season. Write the word vertically, one letter per line. Then, write a poem about your choice, starting each line with the letter listed.

PLAY NOTES

William Shakespeare
1564–1616

Shakespeare wrote plays. To write a play, you need:
1. Setting
2. Time
3. Charcters
4. Plot

Write notes for a play.

1. Describe your setting.

   Where?

2. When?

3. Describe your main character.

   Age:

   Name:

   Traits:

   Interests:

4. Give ideas for your plot.

   On stage is:

   Tell what happens:

What happens next? It's up to you.

2013 Handwriting Without Tears®

CHARACTER SKETCHES

Jef Mallett, the cartoonist, made sketches for the characters in this book. These sketches helped him decide what the final characters would look like.

Make up a character.

Sketch your charac

Name:

Age:

Describe things about your character's appearance.

Size:

Hair:

Clothing:

Describe some other things about your character.

Family:

Pets:

School or work:

Hobbies:

Write a sentence about what makes your character interesting.

CHARACTER SKETCHES

Here is Jef's sketch of Milk Shake Guy. See how the sketch became the final character.

Make up another character.

Name:

Age:

What does your character look like?

Size:

Hair:

Clothing:

Sketch your character.

Tell more about your character.

Family:

Pets:

School or work:

Hobbies:

Adventures:

Make up a comic strip. Draw characters and give them quote bubbles. Fill in the bubbles with what the characters say.
Use a blank sheet of paper.

SHORT STORY NOTES

Mark Twain wrote articles, short stories, and novels. One of his short stories was "The Celebrated Jumping Frog of Calaveras County." To write a short story, focus on one event. Make the event be funny, sad, dramatic, or scary.

Write notes for your short story.

Mark Twain
1835–1910

Title:

Setting:

Event:

Time:

Characters:

What happens in your story? It's up to you. Use your notes to write a one-page story on a separate sheet of paper.

BOOK CASE NOTES

This is not a book report. These are Book CASE Notes.

Cover   Write the title of the book.
Author   Write the author's name.
Start   Copy the first sentence of the book.
End   Copy the last sentence of the book.

For the title, be sure to capitalize the first, last, and important words.

Pick out a book and make your Book CASE Notes.

Sketch the cover.

Cover title:

Author's name:

Starting sentence:

Ending sentence:

BOOK CASE NOTES

Book CASE Notes are great for writing practice. They review both lowercase and capital letters. S-t-r-e-t-c-h this activity for favorite books by telling what happened in the middle. The more you read, the stronger your writing will be!

Pick out a book and make your Book CASE Notes. This time, include what happened in the middle.

Cover title:

Sketch the cover.

Author's name:

Starting sentence:

Middle:

Ending sentence: